NFL TEAM STORIES

The Story of the
DALLAS COWBOYS

By Jim Gigliotti

Kaleidoscope
Minneapolis, MN

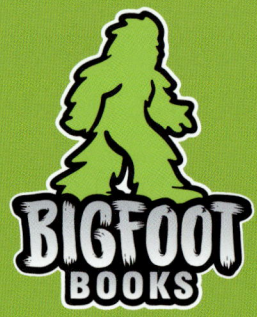

The Quest for Discovery Never Ends

....

This edition first published in 2021 by Kaleidoscope Publishing, Inc.

No part of this publication may be reproduced in whole or in part without written permission of the publisher.

For information regarding permission, write to
Kaleidoscope Publishing, Inc.
6012 Blue Circle Drive
Minnetonka, MN 55343

Library of Congress Control Number
2020933886

ISBN
978-1-64519-226-8 (library bound)
978-1-64519-294-7 (ebook)

Text copyright © 2021 by Kaleidoscope Publishing, Inc. All-Star Sports, Bigfoot Books, and associated logos are trademarks and/or registered trademarks of Kaleidoscope Publishing, Inc.

Printed in the United States of America.

FIND ME IF YOU CAN!

Bigfoot lurks within one of the images in this book. It's up to you to find him!

TABLE OF CONTENTS

Kickoff!.. 4

Chapter 1: Cowboys History 6

Chapter 2: Cowboys All-Time Greats 16

Chapter 3: Cowboys Superstars 22

Beyond the Book.. 28
Research Ninja.. 29
Further Resources... 30
Glossary... 31
Index... 32
Photo Credits... 32
About the Author.. 32

KICKOFF!

America's Team!

Dallas Cowboys fans are everywhere! They don't just live in Texas. They live all over the United States. The team has fans in every NFL city. The fans cheer for the Cowboys even on the road. You'll see the famous Cowboys silver star at just about every NFL game.

Dallas fans have had a lot to cheer about over the years. The Cowboys have had many great seasons. They have won five NFL championships. All that winning has made the 'Boys very popular! That's why they are often called "America's Team." Let's meet the team that a whole country loves!

Texas Stadium opened in 2009. The giant star at the center of the field marks it as the Cowboys' home!

Chapter 1
Cowboys History

Dallas was an NFL **expansion** team in 1960. That is a team that starts from scratch. The Cowboys didn't win a game their first year. But they didn't stay down for long. They had 20 winning seasons in a row starting in 1966! They made the playoffs 18 of those years. They finished in first place 13 times. Seven times the Cowboys played for the NFL title.

Tom Landry was the head coach for all of those great seasons. He was famous for wearing a snappy hat on the sidelines. He had been a great player in the NFL. Landry became an even better coach.

Cowboys action from the famous 1967 "Ice Bowl" game.

FUN FACT
Dallas played Green Bay in the 1967 NFL title game. It was 13 degrees below zero!

The Cowboys made the playoffs for the first time in 1966. Don Meredith was the quarterback. "Dandy Don" was a great passer.

In 1969, Roger Staubach joined the team. He was even better! Staubach was called "Roger the Dodger" because he was hard to tackle. He could run as well as pass. He led the Cowboys to their first Super Bowl win in 1971. Dallas beat the Baltimore Colts 24–3. Staubach had two TD passes in the game.

Duane Thomas in action during Super Bowl VI.

A couple of Cowboys enjoy some Thanksgiving pie.

TURKEY DAY

Thanksgiving is all about food and family. It's also about watching the Cowboys play on TV! The team first played on Thanksgiving in 1966. The Cowboys have played on the holiday every year since 1978. They have won a lot more often than they have lost.

The Cowboys have won the Super Bowl five times in all. After their 1971 win, the next came in 1977. Dallas routed Denver in Super Bowl XII. The Cowboys had the "Doomsday Defense." They **sacked** the quarterback and took the ball away a lot. They were hard to score on. Dallas' offense was good, too. Roger Staubach threw the ball. Tony Dorsett ran it. Drew Pearson was the top pass catcher. The 1977 Cowboys were really a great team!

The Cowboys were even better in the 1990s. They won more than 100 games in that **decade**. They made the playoffs eight of the 10 years. The Cowboys won the Super Bowl in the 1992 and 1993 seasons. They won it again in 1995. That was three Super Bowl wins in four years. They were the first team ever to do that.

Dallas defender Brock Marion dives to tackle a Steelers receiver in Super Bowl XXX.

FUN FACT

The Patriots matched the Cowboys' Super Bowl feat in 2001–2004.

The Cowboys haven't been as good in the 2000s. Jason Garrett was a backup quarterback for the team's Super Bowl-winning teams of the 1990s. He became head coach midway through 2010. Garrett took the team to the playoffs three times. The team did not do well in the playoffs, though.

The Cowboys had a disappointing year in 2019. They started great! They finished not so great. They hired a new coach for 2020. They hope Mike McCarthy can bring the team back to glory!

QB Dak Prescott

TIMELINE OF THE DALLAS COWBOYS

1960

1960: The Cowboys join the NFL.

1966

1966: The Cowboys post the first of 20 winning seasons in a row.

1983

1983: Dallas makes the playoffs for the 17th time in 18 seasons.

1971

1971: The team wins the Super Bowl for the first time.

1995

1995: The team wins the Super Bowl for the third time in four years.

2016

2016: Dallas ties a team record with 13 wins.

2018

2018: Dallas wins the NFC East.

HAIL MARY PASS

Pearson clutched the ball at the end of the Hail Mary play.

The Cowboys stunned the Vikings 17–14 in the 1975 playoffs. The winning score came on Roger Staubach's 50-yard touchdown pass. Drew Pearson caught the pass with only 24 seconds left.

On the play, Staubach dropped back to pass. He threw the ball as far as he could.

"I closed my eyes and said a Hail Mary," he told reporters after the game. A Hail Mary is a prayer. Staubach's prayer was answered. Pearson caught the ball. The Cowboys won the game. A long pass at the end of a half or a game has been called a Hail Mary ever since.

Chapter 2
Cowboys All-Time Greats

It's tough to know where to start with the Cowboys' all-time greats. The team has had many star players! Let's start at the top of the NFL's all-time rushing list. Emmitt Smith ran for more yards than anyone else in league history. Most of those yards came for the Cowboys. Smith was a bruising runner. He wore defenses out. He rushed for more than 1,000 yards 11 seasons in a row. He led the NFL in rushing three years in a row starting in 1991.

Tom Landry was famous for his hat—and for winning. He coached Dallas from 1960 to 1988.

Emmitt Smith

In the 1990s, Emmitt Smith teamed with Troy Aikman and Michael Irvin. They were the "Triplets." Aikman was the quarterback. He was a very smart player. Irvin was a wide receiver. He caught almost anything thrown his way. All of the Triplets are in the Hall of Fame.

The Cowboys also had a great tight end in the 1990s. He was Jay Novacek. Jason Witten took over for Novacek. Witten became the team's all-time leading receiver. He passed stars such as Irvin, Tony Hill, and Bob Hayes to reach the top of the list.

Michael Irvin

Troy Aikman

Many Cowboys from the 1960s, 70s, and 80s are in the Hall of Fame. Roger Staubach also was called "Captain Comeback." The Cowboys were never out of a game when he was the quarterback. Tony Dorsett was the first NFL player ever to run 99 yards for a touchdown. Defensive tackle Randy White was nicknamed "Manster." That was for half man and half monster! Defensive lineman Bob Lilly was "Mr. Cowboy." He never missed a game from 1961–74.

Roger "The Dodger" Staubach

FUN FACT
Before joining Dallas, Staubach served in the U.S. Navy.

COWBOYS RECORDS

These players piled up the best stats in Cowboys history. The numbers are career records through the 2019 season.

Total TDs: Emmitt Smith, 164

TD Passes: Tony Romo, 248

Passing Yards: Tony Romo, 34,183

Rushing Yards: Emmitt Smith, 17,162

Receptions: Jason Witten, 1,215

Points: Emmitt Smith, 986

Sacks: DeMarcus Ware, 117

Chapter 3
Cowboys Superstars

Dak Prescott has been the Cowboys' quarterback since the team **drafted** him in 2016. He was just a fourth-round pick that year. But he wowed the team in **training camp**. He can make plays with his arm or his feet. The Cowboys relied on Prescott more than ever in 2019. He passed for a career-best 30 touchdowns that year. He also passed for 4,902 yards. That was just one yard short of Tony Romo's team record.

FUN FACT

Prescott's full name is Rayne Dakota Prescott—Dak for short!

Ezekiel Elliott is the Cowboys' best running back since Emmitt Smith. The 228-pound back is a tough inside runner. He also has speed to outrun the defense. Elliott led the NFL in rushing his rookie season in 2016. He did it again in '18. Amari Cooper is the team's top pass catcher. He is a big-play wide receiver. He had his best season in '19.

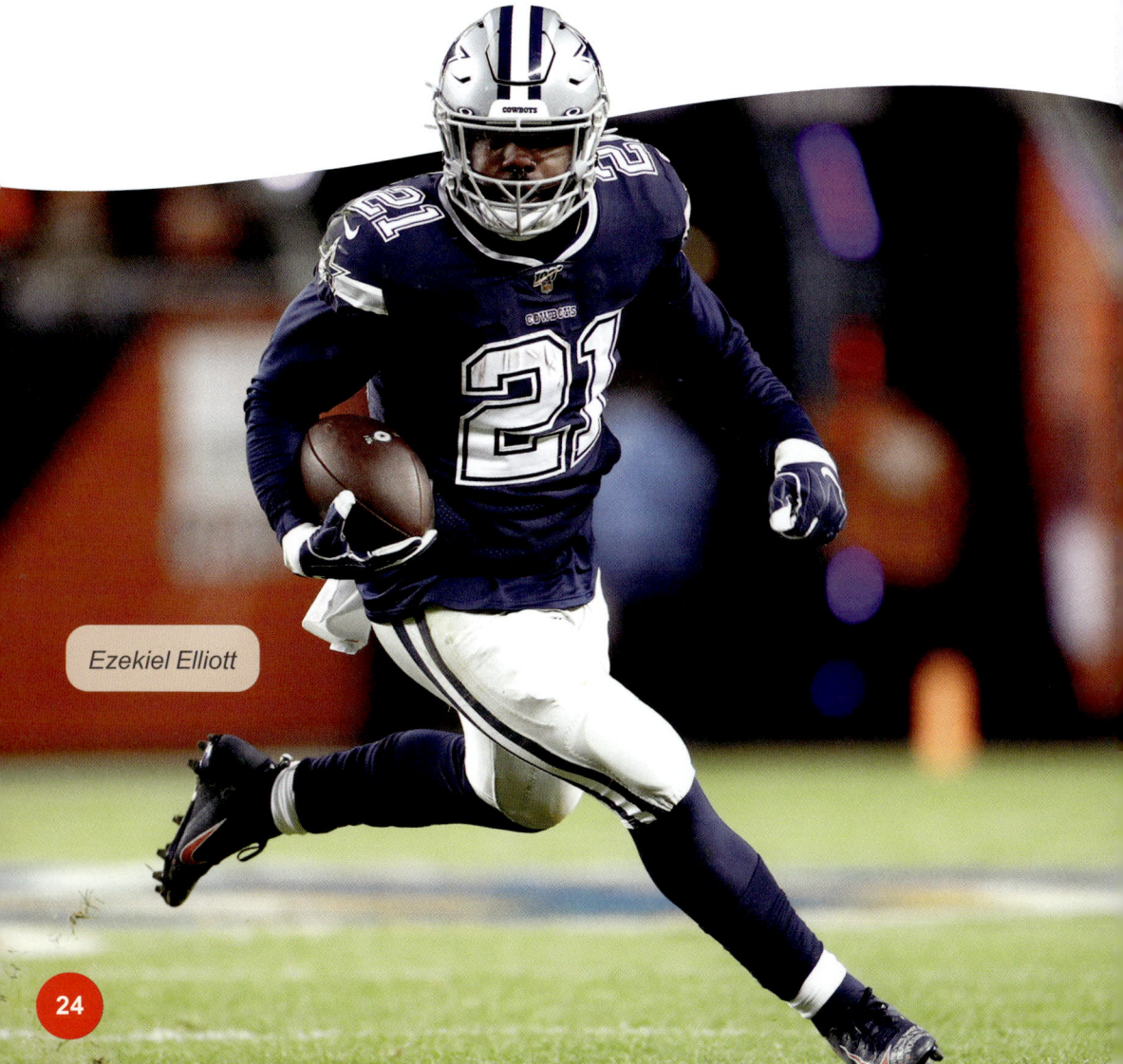

Ezekiel Elliott

Amari Cooper

Prescott, Elliott, and Cooper might be the new Triplets. Does that mean more Super Bowl championships are on the way? Cowboys fans sure hope so!

The Dallas defense is fierce!

Tyron Smith helps protect the Cowboys' quarterback. The big left tackle made the Pro Bowl in the 2019 season. It was his seventh time in a row!

DeMarcus Lawrence and Robert Quinn are pass-rushing ends for the defense. Lawrence led the team with 14.5 sacks in 2017. He added 10.5 in '18. Quinn joined him in 2019. Quinn topped the team that year with 11.5 sacks.

Jaylon Smith usually makes the stop when opponents run the ball. The linebacker is among the NFL's top tacklers. He was in on 142 stops in '19.

Dallas has a long tradition of winning. Fans of America's Team want today's Cowboys to add to that tradition!

BEYOND THE BOOK

After reading the book, it's time to think about what you learned. Try the following exercises to jumpstart your ideas.

RESEARCH

FIND OUT MORE. Where would you go to find out more about your favorite NFL teams and players? Check out NFL.com, of course. Each team also has its own website. What other sports information sites can you find? See if you can find other cool facts about your favorite team.

CREATE

GET ARTISTIC. Each NFL team has a logo. The Cowboys logo shows a silver star. Get some art materials and try designing your own Cowboys logo. Or create a new team and make a logo for it. What colors would you choose? How would you draw the mascot?

DISCOVER

GO DEEP! As this book shows, the Cowboys have fans all over the country. Do some digging and find out more about why that is so. What events led to their national popularity? How did they get the nickname of "America's Team"? What other teams rival them for most fans?

GROW

GET OUT AND PLAY! You don't need to be in the NFL to enjoy football. You just need a football and some friends. Play touch or tag football. Or you can hang cloth flags from your belt; grab the belt and make the "tackle." See who has the best arm to be quarterback. Who is the best receiver? Who can run the fastest? Time to play football!

RESEARCH NINJA

Visit *www.ninjaresearcher.com/2268* to learn how to take your research skills and book report writing to the next level!

RESEARCH

DIGITAL LITERACY TOOLS

SEARCH LIKE A PRO
Learn about how to use search engines to find useful websites.

FACT OR FAKE?
Discover how you can tell a trusted website from an untrustworthy resource.

TEXT DETECTIVE
Explore how to zero in on the information you need most.

SHOW YOUR WORK
Research responsibly—learn how to cite sources.

WRITE

GET TO THE POINT
Learn how to express your main ideas.

PLAN OF ATTACK
Learn prewriting exercises and create an outline.

DOWNLOADABLE REPORT FORMS

Further Resources

BOOKS

Jacobs, Greg. *The Everything Kids' Football Book (Sixth Edition)*. Avon, Mass.: Adams Media, 2018.

Osborne, M.K. *Superstars of the Dallas Cowboys*. Mankato, Minn.: Amicus Ink, 2018.

Ryan, Todd. *Dallas Cowboys (Inside the NFL)*. Minneapolis.: Abdo Publishing, 2019.

WEBSITES

FACTSURFER

Factsurfer.com gives you a safe, fun way to find more information.

1. Go to www.factsurfer.com.
2. Enter "Dallas Cowboys" into the search box and click 🔍
3. Select your book cover to see a list of related websites.

Glossary

decade: a period of ten years. From 1990 to 1999, the Cowboys won 100 games in the decade.

drafted: chosen by an NFL team during the annual event to add college players. The Cowboys drafted wide receiver CeeDee Lamb of Oklahoma with their No. 1 pick in 2020.

expansion: in sports, describe a new team added to a league. As an expansion team, Dallas became the NFL's 13th team.

sacked: tackled the quarterback behind the line of scrimmage. Quinn sacked Tom Brady and the Patriots lost nine yards.

training camp: location of a team's preseason practices and workouts. Dallas holds training camp in California and Texas.

Index

Aikman, Troy, 18
America's Team, 4, 27
Baltimore Colts, 8
Cooper, Amari, 24, 25
"Doomsday Defense," 10
Dorsett, Tony, 10, 20
Elliott, Ezekiel, 24, 25
Garrett, Jason, 12
"Hail Mary Pass," 15
Hayes, Bob, 18
Hill, Tony, 18
Irvin, Michael, 18
Landry, Tom, 6
Lawrence, DeMarcus, 27
Lilly, Bob, 20
McCarthy, Mike, 12
Meredith, "Dandy" Don, 8
Minnesota Vikings, 15
Novacek, Jay, 18
Pearson, Drew, 10, 15
Prescott, Dak, 23, 25
Quinn, Robert, 27
Romo, Tony, 23
Smith, Emmitt, 16, 18, 24
Smith, Jaylon, 27
Smith, Tyron, 27
Staubach, Roger, 8, 10, 15, 20
Super Bowl, 8, 10, 11, 12, 25
White, Randy, 20
Witten, Jason, 18

PHOTO CREDITS

The images in this book are reproduced through the courtesy of: AP Images: Vernon J. Biever 6; Tony Tomsic 8; Sharon Ellman 9; Tom DiPace 10; 14. Focus on Football: 7, 12, 16, 19, 20, 22, 24, 26. Newscom: Roy Carlin 4; Erich Schlegel/KRT 18; Andrew Dieb/Icon SW 25. **Cover photo:** Focus on Football.

About the Author

Jim Gigliotti was an editor at NFL Publishing for many years. Now he writes books for young readers.